To

_____

From

_____

Date

_____

Hope

INSPIRATION FOR EVERYDAY LIFE

MAX LUCADO

THOMAS NELSON

Since 1798

Selections from Max Lucado's writings are taken from:

Facing Your Giants © 2006 by Max Lucado. Thomas Nelson. All rights reserved.
Fearless © 2009 by Max Lucado. Thomas Nelson. All rights reserved.
God Came Near © 1987 by Max Lucado. Thomas Nelson. All rights reserved.
Great Day Every Day © 2007 by Max Lucado. Thomas Nelson. All rights reserved.
In the Eye of the Storm © 1991 by Max Lucado. Thomas Nelson. All rights reserved.
Just Like Jesus © 2007 by Max Lucado. Thomas Nelson. All rights reserved.
Next Door Savior © 2003 by Max Lucado. Thomas Nelson. All rights reserved.
Traveling Light © 2001 by Max Lucado. Thomas Nelson. All rights reserved.

Published in Nashville, Tennessee, by Thomas Nelson. Thomas Nelson is a registered trademark of HarperCollins Christian Publishing, Inc.

Thomas Nelson titles may be purchased in bulk for educational, business, fund-raising, or sales promotional use. For information, please e-mail SpecialMarkets@ThomasNelson.com.

Library of Congress Cataloging-in-Publication Data

ISBN 978-0-7180-9284-9

Printed in China

17 18 19 20 21 RRD 10 9 8 7 6 5 4 3 2 1

Finally, brethren, whatever things are *true,* whatever things are *noble,* whatever things are *just,* whatever things are *pure,* whatever things are lovely, whatever things are of good report, if there is any virtue and if there is anything praiseworthy— meditate on these things.

—Philippians 4:8 (NKJV)

This is more than a silver-lining attitude, more than seeing the cup as half-full rather than half-empty. This is an admission that unseen favorable forces populate and direct the affairs of humanity. When we see as God wants us to see, we see heaven's hand in the midst of sickness, . . . the Holy Spirit comforting a broken heart. We see, not what is seen, but what is unseen. We see with faith and not flesh, and since faith begets hope, we of all people are hope filled. For we know there is more to life than what meets the eye.

— GREAT DAY EVERY DAY

"Do not be anxious about anything, but in everything, by *prayer* and *petition,* with thanksgiving, present your requests to God."

—Philippians 4:6 (NIV)

Don't measure the size of the mountain; talk to the One who can move it. Instead of carrying the world on your shoulders, talk to the One who holds the universe on his. Hope is a look away. Now, what were you looking at?

—TRAVELING LIGHT

*I*t's one of the most compelling narratives in all of Scripture. So fascinating is the scene, in fact, that Luke opted to record it in detail.

Two disciples are walking down the dusty road to the village of Emmaus. Their talk concerns the crucified Jesus. Their words come slowly, trudging in cadence with the dirge-like pace of their feet.

"I can hardly believe it. He's gone."

"What do we do now?"

"It's Peter's fault, he shouldn't have . . ."

Just then a stranger comes up from behind and says, "I'm sorry, but I couldn't help overhearing you. Who are you discussing?"

They stop and turn. Other travelers make their way around them as the three stand in silence. Finally one of them asks, "Where have you been the last few days? Haven't you heard about Jesus of Nazareth?" And he continues to tell what has happened (Luke 24:13–24).

This scene fascinates me—two sincere disciples telling how the last nail has been driven in Israel's coffin. God, in disguise, listens patiently, his wounded hands buried deeply in his robe. He must have been touched at the faithfulness of this pair. Yet he also must have been a bit chagrined. He had just gone to hell and back to give heaven to earth, and these two were worried about the political situation of Israel.

"But we had hoped that he was the one who was going to redeem Israel."

But we had hoped . . . How often have you heard a phrase like that?

"We were hoping the doctor would release him."

"I had hoped to pass the exam."

"We had hoped the surgery would get all the tumor."

"I thought the job was in the bag."

Words painted gray with disappointment. What we wanted didn't come. What came, we didn't want. The result? Shattered hope. The foundation of our world trembles.

We trudge up the road to Emmaus dragging our sandals in the dust, wondering what we did to deserve such a plight. "What kind of God would let me down like this?"

And yet, so tear-filled are our eyes and so limited is our perspective that God could be the fellow walking next to us and we wouldn't know it.

You see, the problem with our two heavy-hearted friends was not a lack of faith, but a lack of vision. Their petitions were limited to what they could imagine—an earthly kingdom. Had God answered their prayer, had he granted their hope, the Seven-Day War would have started two thousand years earlier and Jesus would have spent the next forty years training his apostles to be cabinet members. You have to wonder if God's most merciful act is his refusal to answer some of our prayers.

We are not much different than burdened travelers, are we? We roll in the mud of self-pity in the very shadow of the cross. We piously ask for his will and then have the audacity to pout if everything doesn't go our way. If we would just remember the heavenly body that awaits us, we'd stop complaining that he hasn't healed this earthly one.

Our problem is not so much that God doesn't give us what we hope for as it is that we don't know the right thing for which to hope.

Hope is not what you expect; it is what you would never dream. It is a wild, improbable tale with a pinch-me-I'm-dreaming ending. It's Abraham adjusting his bifocals so he can see not his grandson, but his son. It's Moses standing in the promised land not with Aaron or Miriam at his side, but with Elijah and the transfigured Christ. It's Zechariah left speechless at the sight of his wife, Elizabeth, gray-headed and pregnant. And it is the two Emmaus-bound pilgrims reaching out to take a piece of bread only to see that the hands from which it is offered are pierced.

Hope is not a granted wish or a favor performed; no, it is far greater than that. It is a zany, unpredictable dependence on a God who loves to surprise us out of our socks and be there in the flesh to see our reaction.

—GOD CAME NEAR

Our problem is not so
much that *God* doesn't
give us what we hope
for as it is that we don't
know the right thing
for which to *hope*.

*Y*ou and I live in a trashy world. Unwanted garbage comes our way on a regular basis. . . . Haven't you been handed a trash sack of mishaps and heartaches? Sure you have. May I ask, what are you going to do with it?

You have several options. You could hide it. You could take the trash bag and cram it under your coat or stick it under your dress and pretend it isn't there. But you and I know you won't fool anyone. Besides, sooner or later it will start to stink. Or you could disguise it. Paint it green, put it on the front lawn, and tell everybody it is a tree. Again, no one will be fooled, and pretty soon it's going to reek. So what will you do? If you follow the example of Christ, you will learn to see tough times differently. Remember, God loves you just the way you are, but he refuses to leave you that way. He wants you to have a hope-filled heart . . . just like Jesus. . . .

Wouldn't you love to have a hope-filled heart? Wouldn't you love to see the world through the eyes of Jesus? Where we see unanswered prayer, Jesus saw answered prayer. Where we see the absence of God, Jesus saw the plan of God. Note especially Matthew 26:53: "Surely you know I could ask my Father, and he would give me more than twelve armies of angels" (NCV). Of all the treasures Jesus saw in the trash, this is most significant. He saw his Father. He saw his Father's presence in the problem. Twelve armies of angels were within his sight.

Sure, Max, but Jesus was God. He could see the unseen. He had eyes for heaven and a vision for the supernatural. I can't see the way he saw.

Not yet maybe, but don't underestimate God's power. He can change the way you look at life.

—JUST LIKE JESUS

God will help you *overflow* with *hope* in him through the Holy Spirit's *power* within you.

—Romans 15:13 (TLB)

Heaven's hope does for your world what the sunlight did for my grandmother's cellar. I owe my love of peach preserves to her. She canned her own and stored them in an underground cellar near her West Texas house. It was a deep hole with wooden steps, plywood walls, and a musty smell. As a youngster I used to climb in, close the door, and see how long I could last in the darkness. Not even a slit of light entered that underground hole. I would sit silently, listening to my breath and heartbeats, until I couldn't take it anymore and then would race up the stairs and throw open the door. Light would avalanche into the cellar. What a change! Moments before I couldn't see anything—all of a sudden I could see everything.

Just as light poured into the cellar, God's hope pours into your world. Upon the sick, he shines the ray of healing. To the bereaved, he gives the promise of reunion. For the dying, he lit the flame of resurrection. To the confused, he offers the light of Scripture.

God gives hope. So what if someone was born thinner or stronger, lighter or darker than you? Why count diplomas or compare résumés? What does it matter if they have a place at the head table? You have a place at God's table. And he is filling your cup to overflowing. . . .

Your cup overflows with joy. Overflows with grace. Shouldn't your heart overflow with gratitude?

The heart of the boy did. Not at first, mind you. Initially he was full of envy. But, in time, he was full of gratitude.

According to the fable, he lived with his father in a valley at the base of a large dam. Every day the father would go to work on the mountain behind their house and return home with a wheelbarrow full of dirt. "Pour the dirt in the sacks, Son," the father would say. "And stack them in front of the house."

And though the boy would obey, he also complained. He was tired of dirt. He was weary of bags. Why didn't his father give him what other fathers gave their sons? They had toys and games; he had dirt. When he saw what the others had, he grew mad at them. "It's not fair," he said to himself.

And when he saw his father, he objected. "They have fun. I have dirt."

The father would smile and place his arm on the boy's shoulders and say, "Trust me, Son. I'm doing what is best."

But it was so hard for the boy to trust. Every day the father would bring the load. Every day the boy would fill bags. "Stack them as high as you can," the father would say as he went for more. And so the boy filled the bags and piled them high. So high he couldn't see over them.

"Work hard, Son," the father said one day. "We're running out of time." As the father spoke, he looked at the darkening sky. The boy stared at the clouds and turned to ask about them, but when he did, the thunder cracked and the sky opened. The rain poured so hard he could scarcely see his father through the water. "Keep stacking, Son!" And as he did, the boy heard a mighty crash.

The water of the river poured through the dam and toward the little village. In a moment the tide swept everything in its path, but the dike of dirt gave the boy and the father the time they needed. "Hurry, Son. Follow me."

They ran to the side of the mountain behind their house and into a tunnel. In a matter of moments they exited the other side and scampered up the hill and came upon a new cottage.

"We'll be safe here," the father said to the boy.

Only then did the son realize what the father had done. He had burrowed an exit. Rather than give him what he wanted, the father gave his boy what he needed. He gave him a safe passage and a safe place.

Hasn't our Father given us the same? A strong wall of grace to protect us? A sure exit to deliver us? Of whom can we be envious? Who has more than we do? Rather than want what others have, shouldn't we wonder if they have what we do? Instead of being jealous of them, how about zealous for them? For heaven's sake, drop the rifles and hold out the cup. There is enough to go around.

One thing is certain. When the final storm comes and you are safe in your Father's house, you won't regret what he didn't give. You'll be stunned at what he did.

—TRAVELING LIGHT

But this I call to mind,
and therefore I have hope:
The steadfast *love* of the
LORD never ceases.

—LAMENTATIONS 3:21–22 (RSV)

God's hope *pours* into your world. Upon the sick, he *shines* the ray of healing. To the bereaved, he *gives* the promise of reunion.

Jeremiah was depressed, as gloomy as a giraffe with a neck ache. Jerusalem was under siege, his nation under duress. His world collapsed like a sand castle in a typhoon. He faulted God for his horrible emotional distress. He also blamed God for his physical ailments. "[God] has made my flesh and my skin waste away, and broken my bones" (Lam. 3:4 RSV).

His body ached. His heart was sick. His faith was puny. . . . He realized how fast he was sinking, so he shifted his gaze. "But this I call to mind, and therefore I have hope: The steadfast love of the LORD never ceases, his mercies never come to an end; they are new every morning; great is thy faithfulness. 'The LORD is my portion,' says my soul, 'therefore I will hope in him'" (vv. 21–24 RSV).

"But this I call to mind . . ." Depressed, Jeremiah altered his thoughts, shifted his attention. He turned his eyes away from his stormy world and looked into the wonder of God. He quickly recited a quintet of promises. (I can envision him tapping these out on the five fingers of his hand.)

1. The steadfast love of the Lord never ceases.
2. His mercies never come to an end.
3. They are new every morning.
4. Great is thy faithfulness.
5. The Lord is my portion.

The storm didn't cease, but his discouragement did.

—FEARLESS

*M*artha sat in a damp world, cloudy, tearful. And Jesus sat in it with her. "I am the resurrection and the life. Those who believe in me, even though they die like everyone else, will live again" (John 11:25 NLT). Hear those words in a Superman tone, if you like. Clark Kent descending from nowhere, ripping shirt and popping buttons to reveal the S beneath. *"I AM the Resurrection and the Life!!!"* Do you see a Savior with Terminator tenderness bypassing the tears of Martha and Mary and, in doing so, telling them and all grievers to buck up and trust?

I don't. I don't because of what Jesus does next. He weeps. He sits on the pew between Mary and Martha, puts an arm around each, and sobs. Among the three, a tsunami of sorrow is stirred; a monsoon of tears is released. Tears that reduce to streaks the watercolor conceptions of a cavalier Christ. Jesus weeps.

He weeps with them.

He weeps for them.

He weeps with you.

He weeps for you.

He weeps so we will know: Mourning is not disbelieving. Flooded eyes don't represent a faithless heart. A person can enter a cemetery Jesus-certain of life after death and still have a Twin Tower crater in the heart. Christ did. He wept, and he knew he was ten minutes from seeing a living Lazarus!

And his tears give you permission to shed your own. Grief does not mean you don't trust; it simply means you can't stand the thought of another day without the Jacob or Lazarus of your life. If Jesus gave the love, he understands the tears. So grieve, but don't grieve like those who don't know the rest of this story.

—Next Door Savior

Many are saying of me,

"God will not *deliver* him."

But you, LORD, are a shield

around me, my glory, the One

who *lifts* my head high.

—PSALM 3:2–3 (NIV)

Carlos Andres Baisdon-Niño lay down with his favorite Bible storybook. He began with the first chapter and turned every page until the end. When he finished, he blew his good-night kisses to Mami and Papi, to his three *niñas*, and then, as always, he blew one to Papa Dios. He closed his eyes, drifted off to sleep, and awoke in heaven.

Carlos was three years old.

When Tim and Betsa, his parents, and I met to plan the funeral, they wanted me to watch a video of Carlos." You've got to see him dancing," Tim told me. One look and I could see why. What little Carlos did to the rhythm of a Latin song can't be described with words. He shook from top to bottom. His feet moved, his hands bounced, his head swayed. You got the impression that his heart rate had switched over to his native Colombian beat.

We laughed, the three of us did. And in the laughter, for just a moment, Carlos was with us. For just a moment there was no leukemia, syringes, blankets, or chemotherapy. There was no stone to carve or grave to dig. There was just Carlos. And Carlos was just dancing.

But then the video stopped, and so did the laughter. And this mom and dad resumed their slow walk through the valley of the shadow of death.

Are you passing through the same shadow? Is this book being held by the same hands that touched the cold face of a friend? And the eyes that fall upon this page, have they also fallen upon the breathless figure of a husband, wife, or child? Are you passing through the valley? If not, [these thoughts] may seem unnecessary. Feel free to move on—[they] will be here when you need [them].

If so, however, you know that the black bag of sorrow is hard to bear.

It's hard to bear because not everyone understands your grief. They did at first. They did at the funeral. They did at the graveside. But they don't now; they don't understand. Grief lingers.

As silently as a cloud slides between you and the afternoon sun, memories drift between you and joy, leaving you in a chilly shadow. No warning. No notice. Just a whiff of the cologne he wore or a verse of the song she loved, and you are saying good-bye all over again.

Why won't the sorrow leave you alone?

Because you buried more than a person. You buried some of yourself. Wasn't it John Donne who said, "Any man's death diminishes me"? It's as if the human race resides on a huge trampoline. The movements of one can be felt by all. And the closer the relationship, the more profound the exit. When someone you love dies, it affects you. . . .

Why does grief linger? Because you are dealing with more than memories—you are dealing with unlived tomorrows. You're not just battling sorrow—you're battling disappointment. You're also battling anger.

It may be on the surface. It may be subterranean. It may be a flame. It may be a blowtorch. But anger lives in sorrow's house. Anger at self. Anger at life. Anger at the military or the hospital or the highway system. But most of all, anger at God. Anger that takes the form of the three-letter question—why? Why him? Why her? Why now? Why us?

You and I both know I can't answer that question. Only God knows the reasons behind his actions. But here is a key truth on which we can stand.

Our God is a good God.

"You are good, LORD. The LORD is good and right" (Ps. 25:7–8 NCV).

"Taste and see that the LORD is good" (Ps. 34:8 NIV).

God is a good God. We must begin here. Though we don't understand his actions, we can trust his heart.

—TRAVELING LIGHT

God is a *good* God. Though we don't understand his actions, we can *trust* his *heart*.

"*S*urprise!"

Add to the list of sorrow, peril, excitement, and bedlam the word *interruption*. Jesus' plans are interrupted. What he has in mind for his day and what the people have in mind for his day are two different agendas. What Jesus seeks and what Jesus gets are not the same.

Sound familiar?

Remember when you sought a night's rest and got a colicky baby? Remember when you sought to catch up at the office and got even further behind? Remember when you sought to use your Saturday for leisure, but ended up fixing your neighbor's sink?

Take comfort, friend. It happened to Jesus too.

In fact, this would be a good time to pause and digest the central message . . .

Jesus knows how you feel.

Ponder this and use it the next time your world goes from calm to chaos.

His pulse has raced. His eyes have grown weary. His heart has grown heavy. He has had to climb out of bed with a sore throat. He has been kept awake late and has gotten up early. He knows how you feel.

You may have trouble believing that. You probably believe that Jesus knows what it means to endure heavy-duty tragedies. You are no doubt convinced that Jesus is acquainted with sorrow and has wrestled with fear. Most people accept that. But can God relate to the hassles and headaches of my life? Of your life?

For some reason this is harder to believe.

Perhaps that's why portions of this day are recorded in all the Gospel accounts [Matt. 14:1–33; Mark 6:1–51; Luke 9:1–27; John 6:1–21]. No other event, other than the Crucifixion, is told by all four Gospel writers. Not Jesus' baptism. Not his temptation. Not even his birth. But all four writers chronicle this day. It's as if Matthew, Mark, Luke, and John knew that you would wonder if God understands. And they proclaim their response in four-part harmony:

Jesus knows how you feel.

—In the Eye of the Storm

His pulse has raced.
His *eyes* have grown
weary. His *heart*
has grown heavy.
He *knows*
how you feel.

From the *depths* of his being came a *rush* of emotion that said more than *words.*

Two days ago I read a word in the Bible that has since taken up residence in my heart.

To be honest, I didn't quite know what to do with it. It's only one word and not a very big one at that. When I ran across the word (which, by the way, is exactly what happened; I was running through the passage, and this word came out of nowhere and bounced me like a speed bump), I didn't know what to do with it. I didn't have any hook to hang it on or category to file it under. It was an enigmatic word in an enigmatic passage. But now, forty-eight hours later, I have found a place for it, a place all its own. My, what a word it is. Don't read it unless you don't mind changing your mind because this little word might move your spiritual furniture around a bit.

Look at the passage with me.

Then Jesus left the vicinity of Tyre and went through Sidon, down to the Sea of Galilee and into the region of the Decapolis. There some people brought to him a man who was deaf and could hardly talk, and they begged him to place his hand on the man.

After he took him aside, away from the crowd, Jesus put his fingers into the man's ears. Then he spit and touched the man's tongue. He looked up to heaven and with a deep sigh said to him, *"Ephphatha!"* (which means, "Be opened!"). At this, the man's ears were opened, his tongue was loosened and he began to speak plainly. (Mark 7:31–35 NIV)

Quite a passage, isn't it?

Jesus is presented with a man who is deaf and has a speech impediment. Perhaps he stammered. Maybe he spoke with a lisp. Perhaps, because of his deafness, he never learned to articulate words properly.

Jesus, refusing to exploit the situation, took the man aside. He looked him in the face. Knowing it would be useless to talk, he explained what he was about to do through gestures. He spat and touched the man's tongue, telling him that whatever restricted his speech was about to be removed. He touched his ears. They, for the first time, were about to hear.

But before the man said a word or heard a sound, Jesus did something I never would have anticipated.

He sighed.

I might have expected a clap or a song or a prayer. Even a "Hallelujah!" or a brief lesson might have been appropriate. But the Son of God did none of these. Instead, he paused, looked into heaven, and sighed. From the depths of his being came a rush of emotion that said more than words.

Sigh. The word seemed out of place.

I'd never thought of God as one who sighs. I'd thought of God as one who commands. I'd thought of God as one who weeps. I'd thought

of God as one who called forth the dead with a command or created the universe with a word . . . but a God who sighs?

Perhaps this phrase caught my eye because I do my share of sighing.

I sighed yesterday when I visited a lady whose invalid husband had deteriorated so much he didn't recognize me. He thought I was trying to sell him something.

I sighed when the dirty-faced, scantily dressed six-year-old girl in the grocery store asked me for some change.

And I sighed today listening to a husband tell how his wife won't forgive him.

No doubt you've done your share of sighing.

If you have teenagers, you've probably sighed. If you've tried to resist temptation, you've probably sighed. If you've had your motives questioned or your best acts of love rejected, you have been forced to take a deep breath and let escape a painful sigh.

I realize there exists a sigh of relief, a sigh of expectancy, and even a sigh of joy. But that isn't the sigh described in Mark 7. The sigh described is a hybrid of frustration and sadness. It lies somewhere between a fit of anger and a burst of tears.

The apostle Paul spoke of this sighing. Twice he said that Christians will sigh as long as we are on earth and long for heaven. The creation sighs as if she were giving birth. Even the Spirit sighs as he interprets our prayers (Rom. 8:22–27).

All these sighs come from the same anxiety: recognition of pain that was never intended or of hope deferred.

Man was not created to be separated from his creator; hence he sighs, longing for home. The creation was never intended to be inhabited by evil; hence she sighs, yearning for the Garden. And conversations with God were never intended to depend on a translator; hence the Spirit groans on our behalf, looking to a day when humans will see God face to face.

And when Jesus looked into the eyes of Satan's victim, the only appropriate thing to do was sigh. "It was never intended to be this way," the sigh said. "Your ears weren't made to be deaf; your tongue wasn't made to stumble." The imbalance of it all caused the Master to languish.

So I found a place for the word. You might think it strange, but I placed it bedside the word *comfort*, for in an indirect way, God's pain is our comfort.

—GOD CAME NEAR

Praise be to the God and
Father of our Lord Jesus Christ!
In his great *mercy* he has
given us new birth into a living
hope through the resurrection
of Jesus Christ from the dead.

—1 Peter 1:3 (NIV)

You might hear the news from a policeman: "I'm sorry. He didn't survive the accident."

You might return a friend's call, only to be told, "The surgeon brought bad news."

Too many spouses have heard these words from grim-faced soldiers: "We regret to inform you . . ."

In such moments, spring becomes winter, blue turns to gray, birds go silent, and the chill of sorrow settles in. It's cold in the valley of the shadow of death.

David's messenger isn't a policeman, friend, or soldier. He is a breathless Amalekite with torn clothing and hair full of dirt who stumbles into Camp Ziklag with the news: "The people have fled from the battle, many of the people are fallen and dead, and Saul and Jonathan his son are dead also" (2 Sam. 1:4 NKJV).

David knows the Hebrews are fighting the Philistines. He knows Saul and Jonathan are in for the battle of their lives. He's been awaiting the outcome. When the messenger presents David with Saul's crown and bracelet, David has undeniable proof—Saul and Jonathan are dead.

Jonathan. Closer than a brother. He had saved David's life and sworn to protect his children.

Saul. God's chosen. God's anointed. Yes, he had hounded David. He had badgered David. But he was still God's anointed.

God's chosen king—dead.

David's best friend—dead.

Leaving David to face yet another giant—the giant of grief.

We've felt his heavy hand on our shoulders. Not in Ziklag but in emergency rooms, in children's hospitals, at car wrecks, and on battlefields. And we, like David, have two choices: flee or face the giant.

Many opt to flee grief. Captain Woodrow Call urged young Newt to do so. In the movie *Lonesome Dove*, Call and Newt are part of a 1880s Texas-to-Montana cattle drive. When a swimming swarm of water moccasins ends the life of Newt's best friend, Call offers bereavement counsel, western style. At the burial, in the shade of elms and the presence of cowboys, he advises, "Walk away from it, son. That's the only way to handle death. Walk away from it."

What else can you do? The grave stirs such unspeakable hurt and unanswerable questions, we're tempted to turn and walk. Change the subject, avoid the issue. Work hard. Drink harder. Stay busy. Stay distant. Head north to Montana and don't look back.

Yet we pay a high price when we do. Bereavement comes from the word *reave*. Look up *reave* in the dictionary, and you'll read "to take away by force, plunder, rob." Death robs you. The grave plunders moments and memories not yet shared: birthdays, vacations, lazy walks, talks over tea. You are bereaved because you've been robbed.

Normal is no more and never will be again. . . .

Just when you think the beast of grief is gone, you hear a song she loved or smell the cologne he wore or pass a restaurant where the two of you used to eat. The giant keeps showing up. And the giant of grief keeps stirring up. Stirring up . . .

Anxiety. "Am I next?"

Guilt. "Why did I tell him . . ." "Why didn't I say to her . . ."

Wistfulness. You see intact couples and long for your mate. You see parents with kids and yearn for your child.

The giant stirs up insomnia, loss of appetite, forgetfulness, thoughts of suicide. Grief is not a mental illness, but it sure feels like one sometimes.

Captain Call didn't understand this.

Your friends may not understand this.

You may not understand this. But please try. Understand the gravity of your loss. You didn't lose at Monopoly or misplace your keys. You can't walk away from this. At some point, within minutes or months, you need to do what David did. Face your grief.

—FACING YOUR GIANTS

We, like David,

have two choices:

flee or *face*

the giant.

Why, my *soul,* are you downcast? Why so disturbed within me? Put your hope in God, for I will yet *praise* him, my Savior and my God.

—Psalm 43:5 (niv)

We speak of a short life, but compared to eternity, who has a long one? A person's days on earth may appear as a drop in the ocean. Yours and mine may seem like a thimbleful. But compared to the Pacific of eternity, even the years of Methuselah filled no more than a glass. James was not speaking just to the young when he said, "Your life is like a mist. You can see it for a short time, but then it goes away" (James 4:14 NCV).

In God's plan every life is long enough and every death is timely. And though you and I might wish for a longer life, God knows better.

And—this is important—though you and I may wish a longer life for our loved ones, they don't. Ironically, the first to accept God's decision of death is the one who dies.

While we are shaking heads in disbelief, they are lifting hands in worship. While we are mourning at a grave, they are marveling at heaven. While we are questioning God, they are praising God.

—TRAVELING LIGHT

We know that
suffering produces
perseverance;
perseverance, *character;*
and character, *hope.*

—ROMANS 5:3–4 (NASB)

We don't know how long Jesus wept. We don't know how long David wept. But we know how long we weep, and the time seems so truncated. Egyptians dress in black for six months. Some Muslims wear mourning clothes for a year. Orthodox Jews offer prayers for a deceased parent every day for eleven months. . . .

And today? Am I the only one who senses that we hurry our hurts?

Grief takes time. Give yourself some. "Sages invest themselves in hurt and grieving" (Eccl. 7:4 THE MESSAGE). *Lament* may be a foreign verb in our world but not in Scripture's. Seventy percent of the psalms are poems of sorrow. Why, the Old Testament includes a book of lamentations. The son of David wrote, "Sorrow is better than laughter, for sadness has a refining influence on us" (Eccl. 7:3 NLT).

We spelunk life's deepest issues in the cave of sorrow. Why am I here? Where am I headed? Cemetery strolls stir hard yet vital questions. David indulged the full force of his remorse: "I am worn out from sobbing. Every night tears drench my bed; my pillow is wet from weeping" (Ps. 6:6 NLT).

And then later: "I am dying from grief; my years are shortened by sadness. Misery has drained my strength; I am wasting away from within" (Ps. 31:10 NLT).

Are you angry with God? Tell him. Disgusted with God? Let him know. Weary of telling people you feel fine when you don't? Tell the truth. . . .

David called the nation to mourning. He rendered weeping a public policy. He refused to gloss over or soft-pedal death. He faced it, fought it, challenged it. But he didn't deny it. As his son Solomon explained, "There is . . . a time to mourn" (Eccl. 3:1, 4 NIV).

Give yourself some.

—FACING YOUR GIANTS

Grief
takes
time.
Give
yourself
some.

The LORD delights in those who fear him, who put their hope in his unfailing *love.*

—Psalm 147:11 (NIV)

And *hope* does not disappoint, because the love of God has been *poured* out within our hearts through the Holy Spirit who was given to us.

—ROMANS 5:5 (NASB)